IMBEWU YESINI

IMIBONGO IBHALWE YI-

CYPHER

**THE CAPE YOUTH POETRY HUB
FOR EXPRESSION & RHYTHM**

UHLANGA x LINGUA FRANCA

2016

Imbewu Yesini
© the authors, 2016, all rights reserved

Published in Cape Town, South Africa by uHlanga in 2016
UHLANGAPRESS.CO.ZA

Co-published by Lingua Franca Spoken Word Movement &
the Cape Youth Poetry Hub for Expression and Rhythm (CYPHER)
LINGUAFRANCAPOETRY.CO.ZA
CYPHER.LINGUAFRANCAPOETRY.CO.ZA

This edition is distributed outside of South Africa by African Books Collective
AFRICANBOOKSCOLLECTIVE.COM

ISBN: 978-0-620-73529-2

Cover illustration by Danny 'Mose' Modiba
WWW.MOSEARTSTUDIOS.CO.ZA

Edited by Koleka Putuma and Javier Perez

The body text of this book is set in
SabonNext 11PT on 15PT

CONTENTS

ABOUT THE CYPHER

The Cape Youth Poetry Hub for Expression and Rhythm (CYPHER) is an innovative program whose mission is to equip youth poets with the professional, artistic and personal aptitude to succeed in the field of performing arts and to promote critical thinking, leadership, literacy and empowerment among youth through spoken word education. Through a multilingual and multidisciplinary pedagogy, the CYPHER rests on three pillars: (1) to equip the next generation of performance poets both professionally and artistically; (2) to promote poetry as an educational tool that fosters literacy, public speaking skills, confidence and creativity; and (3) to establish safe spaces for youth voices to be heard and celebrated.

The CYPHER Programme was formed by founding partner Lingua Franca Spoken Word Movement (Pty Ltd), under which it is currently housed and operates. Since its inception, the CYPHER has offered a range of programming to young poets including but not limited to: an International Youth Poetry Exchange; weekly Saturday Workshops; biannual poetry-theatre productions; retreats; one-on-one mentorships; and youth poetry slams. The CYPHER is run by a team of exceptional teaching artists with extensive backgrounds in literature, theatre, and youth development: Lwanda Sindaphi, Koleka Putuma, Javier Perez and Mbongeni Nomkonwana.

The CYPHER caters to youth poets from across Cape Town's diverse communities. The youth contributors to this collection, for example, come from a wide range of areas, including Kraaifontein, Mfuleni, Stellenbosch, Simon's Town, Khayelitsha, Knysna, and Masiphumelele.

For further information, please visit our website:

CYPHER.LINGUAFRANCAPOETRY.CO.ZA

You can also find us on Facebook at:

WWW.FACEBOOK.COM/THECYPHERPOETS

Feel free to contact us by e-mailing:

JAVIER@LINGUAFRANCAPOETRY.CO.ZA

ACKNOWLEDGEMENTS

We wish to extend a special thank you to the District Six Museum Homecoming Centre for all the generous support given to the CYPHER Programme this year. Thank you for hosting our showcasing of *Imbewu Yesini* (the live production) and for providing us with a home throughout the year. As a programme that seeks to reinvigorate the intersections of arts and social justice, we humbly recognise the privilege it has been to operate in partnership with the Museum and its broader transformative work in Cape Town.

We also wish to thank uHlanga for partnering with us to publish our first chapbook. As a Programme that develops young writers and promotes literary excellence, we deeply value your contributions to the South African literary landscape. It is an honour to have our first publication fall under your catalogue.

We would like to further acknowledge John Andelin and Virginia "Ginger" Geoffrey for their generous donation to the CYPHER Programme, without which this chapbook would not be possible.

To all the mentors who have offered their time and energy, there would be no CYPHER without you. A special acknowledgment is due to both Lwanda Sindaphi and Koleka Putuma for brilliantly directing the CYPHER's two productions this year and for your unparalleled emotional investment in this initiative.

To all of the contributing youth poets who appear in this collection, we thank you for inviting us into your lives through your honest and invaluable words. Thank you for being an inspiration to us all and ensuring the future of South African poetry is in good hands.

EDITORS' NOTE

BETWEEN THE POLITICS AND POETICS OF GENDER AND IDENTITY

KOLEKA PUTUMA & JAVIER PEREZ

Often, when we come offstage as poets, there is an expectation that the people we are in public must resemble those we display on stage. Is it a fair expectation? We don't know. Whether or not poems should reflect the ethics of the poet is an ongoing debate in the spoken word community and a conversation that is often left without a conclusion.

When we think of poets, we often think of them as the mirror of/to society; the people who speak truth to power, the ones who sculpt realities through their writing, those who help us see and feel anew about our surroundings and circumstances. It is difficult to imagine the poet shifting other people's perspectives and realities, without their own shifting in the process, unless our politics, opinions or truths as poets are mere aesthetics we are able to switch on and off at our convenience.

Sometimes this may be the case, but when reading *Imbewu Yesini*, you have the sense that there are those among us who still genuinely care about justice, about hope, about equality, love and kindness, those who still yearn to discover more about themselves and about others. Those whose poetics, politics and actions are constantly in critical engagement with one another. The following collection of poetry tells you about a youth in pursuit for self-knowledge, for growth, a youth that is challenging the boxes society has put them in, and a youth that is seeking to unlearn the traumas of its country and biological family. *Imbewu Yesini* is a decolonisation of self and society, firmly rooted in the belief that the personal is indeed political. For, we can only write from a position of what we have learned, what we have seen, and what we hope to learn. This context is one that provides the listener and reader with insight into the kinds of places we come from and, then, the places we wish to still see.

As mentors to these young writers, our task has always been to hold space for these emerging poets to feel safe in authoring their own identities. The task itself requires an intersectional standpoint that renders the space conducive to a more nuanced understanding of the complexities of identity. It is important that youth poets learn early on about the fluidities, overlaps and nuances that exist within – and between – gender, sexuality, race, culture, class and so forth; it is the starting point from which they can accept, celebrate and write themselves and their lived experiences beyond the one-dimensional narratives society will strive to box them into. Acknowledging that no single aspect of identity is more important than another is recognition that all their experiences matter and deserve to be heard. It is the process of dismantling systems of silencing.

Imbewu Yesini was first conceived during a poetry retreat where we facilitated conversations around self-love and, as Lingua Franca's director Lwanda Sindaphi aptly put it, "shifting the focus from Black pain to Black power". The concept was based on the dual task of highlighting individuals' gendered experiences – from the joyful to the traumatic – while simultaneously reimagining how to collectively move forward, as Alice Walker put it, "[in commitment] to the survival and wholeness of an entire people, male and female."

Our youth went on to brilliantly compose a rich range of poems rooted in the personal and of profound social relevance, dealing with topics such as homophobia, mothering, masculinity, period shaming, relationships and much more. There is a beautifully insightful and critically reflective focus on how childhood and adolescence help shape our identities. For example, Lesego Mkhize powerfully revisits how a favourite childhood game for many people actually instills a limited heteronormative understanding of the nuclear family model: "iPoppyhuis had a way of forcing you into a sexuality you didn't always choose." Moreover, Phelisa Sikwata painfully highlights the role of religious institutions in reinforcing a violent fear of those who are allegedly different: "Black. Gay. Women. Our identities behold cages of inferiority in an attempt to tame us." Aviwe Gwele tackles the pressures of masculinity, particularly the myth that men don't cry: "My peers and I emptied sentiments from who we were, like cleaning dirt from seashells To fit definitions of men." While Genevieve Zongolo's resounding words –

"I, woman, am powerful" – celebrates the female body against the backdrop of a society obsessed with Western beauty standards.

Imbewu Yesini is a South African collection, in its tongue, in its rhythm and texture. There is no translation here either. This is important. In a country that is in the process of trying to decolonise its identity, institutions and knowledge production, it's important to produce a work that does not appease the colonised eye or even accommodate it. English has asked of us to do this for a long time. Here, the reader is asked to interrogate what it means to navigate their understanding in a country that is multilingual, in a country that does not always have translations readily available or accessible, one where meaning and relationships slip through the cracks of colonisation, in a country where we miss opportunities because we have not taken the time to learn another's language. It forces you to engage with foreign tongues in between what we have taken for granted as familiar.

When one reads these poems, you get a feeling of where the poet is writing from, and these places are not always geographical, sometimes they are personal and internal. In writing about the experience of being raised in an abusive home with an alcoholic father, Vusumuzi Mpofu preludes his poem 'Family Musical' with "I have only been told one side of the story"; in talking about her relationship with her period and bleeding, Lesego Mhkize reveals, "for as long as I can remember, menstruation in my family has always been narrated this way." *Imbewu Yesini* takes you on this journey, not only of physical locations, but of psychological spaces that have determined the ways in which we write and talk about society and ourselves in relation to others and our upbringing. When Sisipho Makambi writes, "Mother told me to stop looking. Because she was home enough for me, and that nothing was missing", it dawns on you, and in many other lines/stanzas, how much of the self is contextualised by those who raised/birthed us. There is no stronger context than that of our upbringing, and this theme or sense is carried throughout. There is strong presence of the poet's caregiver looming in these pages, even though they are not mentioned by name.

With each poem, one begins to journey back into their own childhood, and the places that influenced one's identity and memory. You began to ask difficult questions about what it means to live and navigate gender and identity between the poetic and personal – and whether there is even a distinction between the two.

ACT I: "THE SEED" – AT SCHOOL

POPPYHUIS | *Lesego Mkhize*

I imagine that
the first child to play ipoppyhuis was Black
so frustrated with the idea of visiting mansions
in a suburb she could never afford to live in
playing guest when she was invited to madams kids' parties
only being invited because she was good at playing guest
for people who would never visit her.
Even White Barbie had a bigger house than hers.
Masidlaleni ipoppyhuise
build a house out of cardboard boxes
plastic bags
sticks and stones.
Black child grew tired of isdudu
and made Weetbix out of old chapped wood.
White stones were crushed into salt.
Mud was turned into chocolate milkshake.
Money was green and made out of leaves.
Yes, money did grow from a tree.
I think the reason why there was always a father
is because boys wanted to play the role
their absent fathers had failed to.
Girls would make rings out of reeds
imagining what life would be like
if their mothers had husbands.
Naturally girls wanted to be like their mothers,
but what happened to the girls that wanted to
be like boys or the boys that wanted to be like girls?
The power of a vagina or penis
had a crazy way of forcing you into a sexuality you didn't always choose.
iPoppyhuis had a way of forcing you into a sexuality you didn't always
    choose.

Ngolala ndenze wawulala
wenze izmanga.
Life lessons always began this way.
Looking back at childhood memories
I've come to realize that ipoppyhuis
taught me izmanga.

UMAMA NDIYAMAZI | *Siphosethu Phikelela*

Umama ndiyamazi
Utata uwaqingqithile amashumi amabini eminyaka wawunabel'uqaqaqa
Ndandingekami nangenja
Ndandisafun'ugaqa ndisosul'imifinya ngolwimi
Anditeketise ndiqhekeke kuvel'izisini
Azingcibe ngebele
Iingono zakhe zazingencinci ukuba zingafikeleli emphemfumlweni
Isithuba esashiywa ngumThembu
Zasivala ndingekaqabuki nokuqabuka
Ndilinqenerha
Ukuba lufuzo ndifuz'utata
Umama wayevuka qho ngentseni aqwab'iintsasa sivuk'isidudu sesibhadla
Ebengazinzi kungekho kuty'embizeni
Ngeentsomi undifundisile
Ngembeko undiqeqeshile
Imizamo yakhe isomelezile
Siyahleka namhlanje xa sicing'emva
Mama
Uyakhumbula ngokuya wawuye emcimbini wasiphathel'inyama sathi sihluthi.
Umkhuluwa wam wayexhele i…
Ndizakuxela kumama
Ndinguntondo, ithunjana kumama notata ndim kuphel'intombazana
Ndisisibane sekhaya
Imbewu yamaMbanjwa
NdinguNomnyamazana ongajikwa nayingqatsini yelanga
Ndishiy'ivumb'elimnandi lomXhosakazi
Ndinganxibanga mbhaco nankciyo
Ndakhawulwa ngumzila wooS.E.K. Mqhayi, Enoch Mankayi Sontonga,
    J.J.R. Jolobe
Amaqhawe!
Nindenz'ibhetyebhetye kuba ndilibhinqa nina
Nizilibele ukuba NONKE
Niphuma kwesisibeleko

BONA BUFELETSWI KESERITI | *Molupi Lepedi*

Bophilo kesemphekgu
Habo mohali huphila kadikgapha
Habo boyi hauluwi
Bona bufeletswi kisiriti

Siqale ngobancoma sabafanisa neentyatyambo kunye nesibhaka-bhaka
Bambi abanye bethu boyisakel kukhetha phakathi kwabo nelanga
Banobuhle beengwenyama zabeqele bosondela basiqhenga sishiyeke
    sizizijunqe

Ivamna ndikuxele boyisakele kundityis'ivamna
Mna nengcinga bekudala siku mzabalazo ndibhal'imibongo
    ndikhawulelane nalemeko
Kwingqondo basivuna ngerhenqe okwamasim'engqolowa siyokuwa ukuze
    intamo ithabathe isihlalo sentloko
Koko mphefumlo bawuqhekez wazinceba
Umthetho ubenzel'iceba bafun'uthabatha isihlalo sobudoda kodwa intloko
    sithi kungako besibon'ubunja.

Eziphekwa ziphakwe ngathi madoda zimanyuku-nyezi
Kuthwa singongatwen isidama isidima sethu sijulw'emaweni
Sikhangela inaliti ebumnyameni siqhoqhiswa ngongena lusini kodwa
    sibambalw'ezweni

Asithathelwa nqalelo intliziyo yintilongo kumahlwili
Zahlinzwa ngetolo ngonoqako kungako ngako neseziba siviwa ngodondolo
Mayijongwe ngeliny'iliso zidwesha lenqumbo
Intliziyo zoxway'imiphako yezinxenxe
Sixhents'emxhobhozweni amabhinq'isityimbisel'umnwe
Kunjenje sizithezele eline nkume

Asiphili ntlango kungoko
Siqonqoza kiminyango yasetshini

Tshini abanye bethu banophulel"imigubasi lonto ayithethi ukuba wonke
    amanene ngamenemene
Masibeni yimbo nomxesibe…

Ngalentiyo iphakathi kwesisbinini
Ngubani omakasolwe kwesithathu abafazi ,amadoda okanye uthixo uqobo
    lwakhe?

SALTY WATER | *Aviwe Gwele*

At an early age
I learned how to be a storm,
a man staffed with a boy carrying salty seas with his eyes.
My actions are like waves which never felt the comfort of a shore.

I would come home crying.
Auntie would give me a hiding: go back and fight,
your genes aren't fused with femininity,
don't be a sissy.

Hanging on the verge of emotion,
I never learned to rain, holding the salty water too long.
Now I'm a flood in motion learnt how to deny myself the pleasure of
    crying.
My cheeks never felt the baptism in ocean overflowing with tears.
I've never been resurrected out of shame.
I carry a hunchback of expectations like a backpack filled with seashells.

Amongst peers fighting was like riding violent waves to manhood.

They monitored who would cry first,
whose nose would be like sea running blood.

My peers and I emptied sentiments from who we were, like cleaning dirt
    from seashells
to fit definitions of men.
Men don't cry but what do we do when no one's in sight?
We play wrists with razors,
go head to head with guns on our heads,
so to expose the softness held in our beneath our skulls.

Us boys resemble sponges:
we absorb all pain
until one day,
we
squeeze
and
we
all
drown.

ACT II: "THE WATERING" – AT CHURCH

UNREAD NOTE ON THE CLOSET DOOR | *Phelisa Sikwata*

Common errors we have painted between our fingers.
Identical mistakes we have skins drenched in.
Tortured bodies we have used to sing in premises of uneasy gods.
We are afraid:
not to give birth to mother made children;
afraid to sleep in unlocked rooms;
to take a walk at night
scared that that guy who saw
you kissing your sis'bae, might have the urge to force in his 4-5.
We are afraid of being blood-related, ridiculed for being us!
Black. Gay. Women.
Our identities behold cages of inferiority in an attempt to tame us to feel
small in a world formed by our filth.
We secretive same-sex lovers soak our top in bottom lips.
We make love with no sin in mind.
Our need for love make us innocent ghouls, in a world filled with faulty
angels.
Mothers of my kind invite in our rooms animated frair to wash away the
spirits that gather in us.
They might come again to pray for me… so I'll just act as if I'm "healed"
hide my mother's daughter from her.
Every now and then, when no one is looking
I'll go unpack myself from that suffocating closet
wear myself for a stolen minute or two.
Before I leave my room though,
I undress myself,
neatly fold her in that dark corner and
walk away with a religiously sowed smile.
My ears have gotten used to these praising verses of an uneasy god –
His hatred right, our honest love wrong.
My ears have gotten used to being accidentally enlightened by carelessly-
dropped words by siblings:
honestly, I have no problem with them as long I'm not related to one.

My invisible tears water my smile into a grin,
since the one they are speaking of befriended my skeletons.
This hatred formed fear, became part of on-my-way-out routine
where I peel off my skin to leave it unwashed
(scented with past affairs, softened by secrecy).
There are many of my kind in my family who will pretend to walk
     mindlessly past
this 'unread note' cause it's quite cynical.
While many continue to hide their wrinkled selves under influential
black blouse, scarlet scarves with gold rings…
Head off to church.
Cause it's the right thing to do.

STRETCHMARKS AND PROPHECIES | *Sisipho Makambi*

There's many places we could've come from.
But I'm not certain becausemy origin is a confusing contradiction.
Mother says my bones were carved and put together by the Word.
Sometimes when my backbone is visible and upright I disagree out loud
    and whenever she calls me a blasphemer I tremble and my bones shake
    and I think that maybe God is a sangoma,
who had to resort to wearing white robes when primates discovered
    shaving, grew a pair and a backbone.
But seriously, what other places could we have come from?
It's really hard to tell, cause there were no street names inside my mother's
    belly.
Even the soil I was apparently moulded from was eroded from rocks that
    used to shelter cavemen which had no address so I'm not quite certain
    about my origins.
Apparently my name was carved in one of his books before I came to be
    and I was woven together in the depths of the earth.
Personally I know no deeper sanctuary than a womb.
Picture it as a thread going into the hole, moving in and out and stitching
    together a wonderful creation
inside my mother's womb.
Now Mother is a creator but refuses to acknowledge it.
She will not stand up for herself.
She does not believe in evolution.
She is also quite ashamed of her stretch marks, unaware that they're
    scriptures of prophecies I wrote before I was born.
She stopped dragging me to church cause she was tired of seeing me
    represent evolution in the house of God.
During sermons I slouched and towards the end I was awake and upright.
Mother is a creator but she still refuses to acknowledge it.
Gives credit to a man in the sky, I've always wondered where my father was.
He's hiding behind the clouds while an earth full of his kids wait for him
    in agony.
Mother still does not believe me.

UNTAMED | *Genevieve Zongolo*

My grandparents say that education has killed me and resurrected
a modern impresionalist, who walks contradictory to their traditional ways.

You are too forward, too vocal, unruly and not submissive as a Xhosa
    woman should be.
You act like a man!

A Xhosa woman is dignified, no man will ever marry you!
They believe that if a woman wears a cloth that divides her thighs
she proclaims she's a man. They dressed me in long robes so I may
look dignified.

Perhaps the issue was not the clothes, but the vocal woman in me
they are trying to tame by selling me lies: we are grooming you to be
    someone's wife,
you will someday bear children and build a home, as if that all I'll ever
be good for.

The silence of vocal women who have been tamed like I am enters me
like a spirit that awakens the slumbering Khoisan residues pumping in
    my veins, leads me to dance, in the dusty roads of the Karoo, 'til dust
    stands in ovation
rejecting and shaking off all those strings of lies tied around my head.
Call me Xhoisan.

The San woman that can't be tamed by Xhosa traditionalists.
The Xhosa drum tickles my eardrums, the San melodies tickle my soul.

I can never be tamed.

NDIXOLELE QAMATA | *Palesa Mohlala*

Ndixolele Qamata
Tswarelo Kgoshi ya phula
Ndiphila kwilizwe lenkululeko nkululeko leyo ekhulula amasiko
I have forgotten the dense scent of imphepho,
I cast demons away with my faithless polished accent.
My hands are numb to the defense mechanism of sticks and stones
I have traded them for steel-bar fences
These were not ideals by my kind
I can tell because as time passes,
barbed wires restrict the perimeter of land
Me between Constantia on weekdays and Khayelitsha on weekends.
    (Existing)
Perimeter of humanity
Me, suggesting a mere greeting during the week (Existence)
Perimeter of self-consciousness.
Mislead. (Extinction)
Ha ke toma ho butsisha hoba kannete nna ke mang
The possibilities are endless
Breastfed by one culture, sandwiched between two
My name is overweight
And I'm weighed down, perplexed by this concept of 'define and empower'
only because we're redefining customs with a little bit of individuality and
    more of our preference
Solely based on #hashtag asinavalo.
I have uvalo.
Me between Constantia on weekdays and Khayelitsha on weekends – uvalo
Me suggesting a mere greeting during the week – uvalo
Misled – uvalo
I don't want to be categorized down under one title,
because I choose to wear all of me
My hair, my skin, my femininity, my flaws.
I am all cultures I intersect with,

from my Afro to the taste of potjiekos in the afternoon (Awe) down to
    Woodstock collecting Sari's for heritage day, snacking on hot halaal
    samoosas fresh outta Athlone.
I am all experiences I have endured and enjoyed.
I just can't exercise my choices yet
so allow me:
Some days to sleep like a feminist in a king-size mattress
to hoe around politics
lingering to the sound of Mbuyiseni Ndlozi economic singing, costing all
    sleepist to rise up.
Allow me to jump and jive like a traditionalist for an hour because
Beyoncé got nothing on my aunt's thundering, drumbeat heels.
Our Freedom Charter has not only fooled us to being free from the system
kunxityiswe amasiko lenkululeko siyithenjisiweyo.

ACT III: "THE BLOSSOMING" – AT THE FAMILY TABLE

MY FAMILY'S MUSICAL | *Vusumuzi Mpofu*

I have only been told one side of this story…
When the tavern's jukebox had stopped playing
he would come home drunk
make his own music
using my mother's body as an instrument
beating her bleeding hide
like a drumplayer possessed by melodies screeching from vocal chords
cries
calling neighbours as audiences to a musical staged behind closed curtains
    and locked doors
The production always ended with him singing hymns of apologies
using mother's love for music
convincing her to stay
until she grew tired of dancing to sorrowful symphonies
departed with lyrics of scars on her body
and a boy on her back
I was once a hunchback, weighing mama down
Sometimes, these days I feel like a scar –
a constant reminder of her mellow past.
Just like my father, I have also fallen in love with music
The difference between us is the genres we jam to
I love punch lines and bars
he used to punch lines, on her body when he came home late from bars
My childhood is like a torn-apart songbook
lacking tunes celebrating happy times
I am decomposing these sad rhythms
re-learning the music made by my parents before the chaos began
I am going back to a time when the only beating she knew
came from her youthful heart

as his hands were still learning her body instrument like a pianist making
    melodies
I want to re-learn the high-pitched laughters composed as I attempted my
    first steps
stumbling like my drunk father
trying to dance to the tavern's jukebox
before he came back home
and, my family's musical began

THE PERIOD WE DO NOT TALK ABOUT | *Lesego Mkhize*

No baby
your body is not hurt:
a girl has died inside of your body,
she is simply bleeding herself out.
She needs to leave this way or the blood will rot inside of you,
and you will smell of a dead girl even when you are a woman.
This is how you can be both alive and ghost all at once.
No female wants to smell of a dead girl, especially when she is a woman
This is the period we do not talk about.
For as long as I can remember, menstruation
in my family has always been narrated this way.
Menstrual blood is dirty.
We are told to
stay away from sharks disguised as innocent boys.
Sharks love blood,
but not you,
and your blood will be the reason why sharks are
attracted to you. So if you ever get raped it's your own fault,
because menstrual blood is dirty!
It is polluted with chapped pieces
of your heart –
that's why it has to leave your body.
Even the walls around your vagina cannot contain it.
Every month
for seven days
I am bleeding another woman out.
My circumcision period does not end.
How do you expect me to stay the same?
And why do boys not bleed like we do?
Why do they not bleed into men?
These boys that climb mountains to find their hidden
manhood, sometimes only to lose it in the streets.
I wish someone could've said to me instead:

No baby
your body is not hurt:
you are bleeding from a wound that does not heal.
Stop stitching up your womanhood,
covering it up with band-aids and apologizing
as if bleeding makes you hurt.
This is the period we do not talk about.

WAR | *Aviwe Gwele*

When I showed up
Aunty spoke loud like a bullet engaging her companion:
Look at him. Whose son is he?
The lady perused my face like a rare artifact.
Her response rolled like a naked hand grenade, affirming the truth:
The grave might have claimed his father, but his image is hung alive on his face.
Heredity drenches on his eye sockets.
Being likened to my father threw me in a puzzle of smoke.

He was a stranger attached to an idea I played with
whenever peers bragged about their complete families.

My toddlerhood claimed for itself a portrait of him when we played together.

He ran in front of me. I mimicked his running staggering
learning how to walk bare as target practice to be shot at when he disappeared.

I do not remember arriving to his arms
like I remember mother selling Russians for 7,50 so I could get shoes for
     primary.

I have one incomplete memory in a chamber as BOOM! shot at whoever
     questions me about him.
Not the part he would be around when the household sang waqingq'
     umntwana.

I'm a gene worn in camouflage, torn from the battle he lost to my mother.

My heart lies as a casualty in my chest.
His departure introduced me to a stepdad: a policeman,
whereas daddy was a soldier.

Mother loved militant men who pinched her with handcuffs
as she remained helpless a subject to their law of abuse.
Eventually living without a male figure were the remains we collected in
    recollecting our lives.

At granddad's house everyone was female except him, my three cousins and I
I knew to be a man meant tying granddad's sandals,
embody his dragging walk between lines of plantation freeing seeds from
    his hands.

We would awaken dawn at cocks' crow to tend fields.
In our breaks granddad fit his entire life in conversation

about his father who was a brick man and a field-tender
and how we traced the paths they led.

I contemplated lies I would tell my kids when they inquire about my father.

MAMELA NONTOMBI | *Siphosethu Phekelela*

Mamela Nontombi
Mamela khe ndikuphokozele kulamav'entombendal'enyawo zinamasa,
Ndidlule kulendlela ndihamba ndisandlala bendixavatha
kakad'undwendwe lunyathelwa nangabantwana
Mamela
Okwetshemba, bokufakamatshona bakugqib'ukuchamela
Bakuchithele ngaphandle
Lo ngumdlalo'ngasoz'uw'qonde ekuqaleni
Bakuzobel'ikamv'eliyokoyoko
Wakuw'emgibeni
bakufunx'incindi bakushiy'uligobhogobho elingafunwa nangooNgantweni.
Mamela.
Andisozendik'qhathe kumnand'udlala
Xa nityumzana'mathumba nichebana'maduma
Ninyumbazan'ugigithek'akuyifaka
Andisoze ndik'fihlele kub'hlungu'kohlukana
Uzigqibel'uyinkosazana wothuke sel'ungumngqusho nto
    ley'angasoz'alal'ety'eyon'umhla nezolo
Mamela
Xa ndikuqoshelisa andikumoneli ngeyaviwa nguEf'emyezweni
Ndikhusel'isdima sakh'ukuze naw'ubengumnt'ezizweni
Uzukhe uyek'uziphatha mgqutsub'okwentwal'eskhaka
Ndiyathemba sivene

MAMA AFRIKA | *Palesa Mohlala*

I've seen melanin caress melanin
Mama you adore us
I've seen melanin augment melanin
Mama you built us
I've seen melanin love queer
Mama I know you're queer
But lover, mama's lover questions queer
He buckles his belt up high above his patriarch belly
He protects mama
sometimes
Other times he doesn't want to see mama tired in the kitchen
He doesn't want to see mama's salary
He doesn't want to see brother sweep in the kitchen
He tells brother he's a man
I see the men walk all over mama
Brother doesn't sweep kitchen floor
Brother doesn't see mama tired in the kitchen.
Brother feels proud
Brother is a man
Brother is changing the world, his world, revolution
My world is not changing
Brother's revolution takes up too much space in Mars – Venus is
        claustrophobic
Suffocating under his patriarchy
Soon I won't meet the requirements to sing along his army to protest
Soon I won't have the strength to push Mr Rhodes down with brother
Because brother , just like mother's lover, won't see past his consciousness
        that I am not safe walking alone
Mama sees all the men walk all over me
Brother doesn't stop the men walking over me
Brother holds a silent protest, sh
"You shouldn't have worn that, you know boys will always be boys."
I dress like them now.

But Brother's army orbits insults at me
Brother's army think they can fix me
Brother's army is fixed. Consciously silent about my oppression
Brother's revolution takes up too much space in Mars – Venus is
    claustrophobic
Our milky way has turned sour
But brother don't pull your face like that
We can always root our feet on gravity
Brother tell your army that you are orbiting, shifting, evolving, on a galaxy
    creating space for all stars to flare

ACT IV: "SHEDDING THE PETALS" – IN THE SELF

VUSA UMUZI | *Vusumuzi Mpofu*

Mother was eighteen years old when she discovered a magic lamp,
contemplated rubbing it
in hopes of making her wishes come true. Didn't.
Feared the world no longer believes in magic,
hid the lamp within her body.
Concealed in her womb, it swelled
inflating her stomach.
She believes in magic.
Rubbed her swollen lamp of flesh nightly for nine months hoping for a
    miracle to happen
Finally!
Wednesday 11 June 1997,
Genie popped out of mother in the form of a child.
A moment to wish, she said "…vusa umuzi…"
My name is magic fused with life-purpose,
meaning build home.
Mama, your wish is my command.

INGXOXO MPIKISWANO | *Molupi Lepedi*

Ndiboleken'idivedi ndombathe.
Ndithabath'iqula kobuqilimia.
Ndiyoqonda kwiincali,icula zencuba buchopho
zindicocisel'icubeko ihlal'echininika kwincinga.
Zeziyithathe ziyicocisa ziyicacisa lentsinda badala yoba kutheni hili
    uphum'ezincongolweni.

Mvanje ndivamis'ungakwazi uxhel'exhukwana.
Ndikuv'ukhasa uxhentsa, uxhuma kwigumbi lengcinga.
Kwelengcinga wena amaxhwele na maxhalanga nindilandela ngamazembe.

Ndikuve mzimba umfimfithek ushike uligobho gobho
imeko zamaxongo nexhego lingekawurhabuli nomthendeleko
Yanga ndingakuvul'incango sfuba nsikuthavathe ntliziyo alsivul'ingxoxo
    mpikiswano
Kuthe ufake kwesiziba sothando mna ndiyayizonda lentlalo
indivimb'ingqiqo

Uhamba ngogaga uxel'inyoka, enyuk'emthin kodwa ayinanyawo.
Wancam wakhula ngenkxa yokunyoluka
Ntliziyo yanga ndinga balekel kwelamrhanugha.

Themba likamadosini ndilincwabil'emadlakeni akanasizi nalusini
intsizi iyihlekil'ntsini
koluqatso lothando siyofika entanjeni
Ukuba besidalelenwe intliziyo ngezisa gangxene uthando ngelisa
    nconywaubuhle oboqith'igolide nesilivere

Ndidandathekil ndivul'ingxoxo kwingqondo ndixakwe kubheka ekunene
    okanye ekunxele inxaki zixananazile.
Unxunguphalo luthi tarhu emphefumlweni kudalek'umonakalo
    etliziyweni.
Uyandifikela ethongweni

Leyoyis'amaduna namathokazi maziyilwe izilo zezilwanyani ukuba
olu lubizo mandabathisw'ibhayi ndixhelwe ibhokwe ndinkwe
umkhombandle ndiyinike inkonde nenkondekazi ziyixove ziyibhaka
zibhake zixov lenxuba kaxaki impendulo ithi elidonga ayisilo lwakho
kanti asidalelenwe

FAMILIAR STRANGER | *Sisipho Makambi*

I've tried running from myself so many times you can see the scars I got
from a far distance.

Some of them come from teaching myself how to ride a bicycle so it would
never be too obvious there was no father figure around.

Bicycle rides were a taste of liberation. The wind would gently brush my
skin, reminding me of my mother's embrace that my brother now
owns. I would prefer the tarred road grazing my skin and the bicycle
chain sinking it's teeth into my ankles than be at home.

Home felt as if it was missing something.

A few paintings and a vase for the flowers.

I would picture riding those borrowed bicycles, with home disappearing
behind me until I got to this huge lost and found box.

I never got to the part where I found the things we had lost.

In my head I imagined pulling out a carpet that said welcome.

Its bristles would scratch playfully on my skin.

Mother told me to stop looking because she was home enough for me
and that nothing was missing.

She does not know that my bones have been reciting my father's name
since I was born.

That they break only to be put together again by the hope of one day
taking him by the hand and bringing him back home.

My blood cells join together like constellations only to point me in his
direction.

I imagine running into my father's arms and my blood rushing throughout
my body to spread the good news.

The lost has been found.

The home has been furnished.

This is all in my imagination.

All I can carry with me is the fact that I am bone of your bone and flesh of
your flesh.

I've tried being cliché, acting as if your name left burn marks on my tongue.

The truth is that my mother punched these holes on my tongue so that whenever I spoke of you, your name would drown in my saliva and be buried inside my oesophagus.

Sometimes when the cracks in the walls got too visible or the roof was falling apart and my mother could no longer hold it up I would exhume you, but you'd go right back into your grave because she could not bear the stench.

To her you were a decaying carcass.

I still tell myself you're just delaying the process.

Maybe when you're ready you'll dig yourself out of that grave and come back home.

But Mother will not have ghosts inside her house.

I want to remind her I am bone of your bone and flesh of your flesh and that I have enough soul and physical capacity for both me and you.

Naivety has got me rolling in its palms.

I want warmth and presence from a ghost.

I want to bring strangers into my mother's house.

Longing has got me rolling in its palms.

Embalmed in lotions of desperation.

I am still bone of your bone.

And indeed, flesh of your flesh.

CRAZY NUTS, THUNDER BOLTS | *Lesego Mkhize*

Growing up I have always been hit with the Bible on my mouth.
So, how do I tell my mother that I think she is praying to a borrowed God?
How do you fix broken faith?
When conversations with God feel like consultations
and I am broke.
I can no longer afford this God
I have never been able to afford Him
only borrowing the Bible and Christianity
hoping one day it will be mine.
The pulpits at church have turned into banks.
Pastors have become loan sharks.
I am tired of praying for something I can never keep.
I am a dead person attending church just not in a casket.
I haven't been to church for months.
I am a tool
spade corroded
blunt axe.
I do not know how to fix things like
pipes that have ruptured
bursting open.
I am the bursting open.
I feel it sometimes in my anger
like rupturing guts
intestines turned inside-out
side of my body I am spilling bile
and frustration.
Whenever this happens I feel the church
I have built with my mother
beneath my bed crumbling.
Lately being human, writer, student and woman is hard.
Whenever I go home I have to be something else
other than my name.
My name doesn't deserve to be a part of this body

It doesn't carry enough weight.
Eventually when I am asked this question
I gratify this body with titles that
will make my aunts swallow me in conversation faster.
I want to tell them I am a tool.
But what good is a tool if it's not fixing?
On my worst days I am demolishing
I cover my adulthood in dust
hoping to baptize myself back into childhood.
The lawyer I wanted to be
when I grow up is still a child
only in an adults body.
I do not understand this adulthood.
All I want to be now is alone.
I want to soak myself in red wine
until I taste the maturity on my skin.
Maybe then mother will drink me like a grown up.
Mother has seen my insides whenever I spill.
She has tasted my expired patience accidently slipping off my tongue.
My words like clenched fists have left blood in her mouth before.
I have watched mother's broken heart bleed through her mouth.
I have tried to hammer apologies into her chest
hoping to fix her broken heart.
I am not the cardiologist she wanted me to become.
I do not know how to fix broken hearts.
On my worst days I am demolishing
I turn the house
into a construction site.
I have watched the unmarried women in my family collapse
whenever I unearth the buried corpses beneath the dining room carpet.
The ceiling is cracking from being cemented with lies.
I do not build
only destruct.
The children have started asking about their fathers
who have accidently enveloped themselves into another woman's thighs
This is how I know that not all males are delivered.

Mails sometimes get lost in the post.
At worst being the head of a house
with no brain.
The women in me want to become men
and father the children in my family
marry the women with these children
so they will stop fathering the wrong men.
I am tired of attending funerals during family gatherings
for men who are still alive
but dead as fathers.
Spade corroded.
Blunt axe.
To be a tool is not easy
People think you're good at fixing
life
But who fixes the broken tools?

MY SISTER IN ME | *Phelisa Sikwata*

If you would look into my soul
you will see
an explosive box of a soul that stores utter love,
naive joy skipping around like a little girl, a sence of wonder – that
of a newborn
soaked in a bath of raging loneliness
needs of nonsense
ecstasies of hatred
my deprived acceptance of resentment;
my butterfly spirit contained in fragile glass jars
my womb drenched in filth – cause the womenhood that I await
I'm not deserving of.
If you would look in my soul you'll see utter love
that is rejected by religious beliefs
naive joy skipping around like a little girl's memories when she tries
to forget those nights her father was the cause of her tears
a sense of wonder that of a newborn
trying to understand why she is not loved nor wanted.
If you would look in my soul
you'll see my customed saddening reality.

NDAPHULUKWA | *Sisipho Makambi*

Nosipho, khawuyovalela iigusha ebuhlanti mfondin.

Wena Ntsika, vala lo milenze, inkwenkwe ayihlali olohlobo.

Khona ungumfana onjani ongakwaziyo upheka, umane utshisa iimbiza,
umosha ezinkuni zivelo gawulwa nguDade wenu.

Khawutsho khona, ucinga la ntombi yasebaThenjini izakumfuna umyeni
olivila nje ngawe, awukwazi nopheka isidudu esi, hayi.

Jonga udade wenu, bonke abafana bale lali bayamwela, bavele babe
zizidenge bakubona uncumo lwakhe.

Phof ke yimfuzo.

Mna noDadobawo wakho, sasiziz'bethi.

Ithi ingulo, ibengu lo.

Tshin kwedini!

Ndithi la mfana kaXolani ebezozicelela umtshato.

Wakhe wayiva phi?

Umfana ozicelela umtshato?

Hayi, inene!

Kugos' okwaphukayo.

Uyabona ngomso oku, ndiya Kula lali ingaphesheya komlambo, ndiyoxoxa
ngendaba yolotyolwa kwakho.

Uyihlo lo, kufuneka andiphekele la nto yam ndiyithandayo, olule
neempahla zam zehambo.

Wena ke nyana, ndifuna ezambiza neezabhekile zimenyezele, zixel'
impandla kaMam' Mabhengeza.

Ungaqhweshi, ndiyakwazi ngothanda unomchesi kude kutshone ilanga.

Izibane azinakukhanya Umfana engaphandle kwamasango.

Ntsika!

Khawumamele, uzakubakhulisa njani abantwana xa unje.

Lo nto ingathi uyakhula.

I, WOMAN | *Genevieve Zongolo*

I, woman, was made out of the rib of man
just below his heart
This temple is an instrument of goodness
My eyes are made to perceive the best in people
This mouth is to speak good to you
and of you, engraved in perlites of my tongue
is the power of peace and war
I
I, woman, am good.
My smile stretches like a cloudless sky
My bosom is made for solice
and comfort my thick arms
head shield in embrace
My hands are made to nurture nations
The strength in my arms is like that of soldiers
prepared for war
My palms hold the despaired
and fingers encage
I, woman, am grounded
My waist an anchor, when your arms surround and interlock
around this waist you stand rooted
firm and immovable
My womb is a haven for unborn generations
nations of greatness
These legs are pillars and feet a foundation to keep
this temple stands unshaken
I, woman, am powerful

READY TO LOVE | *Phelisa Sikwata*

I do not live darkness of blasphemous tales
Nor do I bath in waters filled by snakes with slithering tongues of lies
But I must say, I have missed those warm nights meant for my heart
Long I have waited to be cleansed with waterfall kisses
to breakdown this wall stoned with memories of hurtful experiences
I am ready to erase these lines, roughly stained in me
     during moments I mistaken as loving intimacy
I am ready to soak my feet in liquids of ones heart
     Can somebody, anybody take time to create this gemstone to
                  excite my women-ness beings
To glorify me with lusty melodies of a saxophone
            I want to take a journey
To place my very own heart in the hands of another
Stand barenaked
letting the breeze make itself at home at the split-ends of my hair
It's about time
     hope has found me
How beautiful this feels
I am ready to love whole-heartedly
Yes, I finally said it
I am ready to fly high to the sky
Heavenly father take this heart of mine and find its other half
I am ready for love, Ready to be loved, Ready to love
My heart awaits to be Jazzed through Hallways of lyrical notes
Written to experience me from my cherry lips to my African Golden thighs
LOVE is what I'm ready for!

UYIMBEWU | *Siphosethu Phikelela*

Uyimbewu
Umhlaba asinawo wathathwa ngolunya kooBawomkhulu
Yiyo lonto ndakutyala
Ngaphakathi, ezantsi ebushushwini besizalo
Ndakwenzel'isixeko
Ndakuhlakul'ukhula
Ndikuncenceshela ngamanz'othando
Ndandingekakuboni ngelenyama
Kodwa ndandisazi ukuba ndityal'imbewu ehlumayo
Imbewu Yesini
Imbewu ezakwanda ilibuyisele kubanikazi elilizwekazi

"Ugotywa uselula, inimba mayibenye bafazi"
Batsho kanye xa ndinqumka isisu sinditsheqa butyani
Ukuba kwakusiya ngam ngendakufukama naphakade kwesisixeko
Iinkqwithela zesini zikhuhle mna
Izantyalantyala zeenyembezi zikhukhulise mna
Ndingunyoko
"Igqabi aliweli kude emthini walo"

Ndizalwa yimbeko, intobeko nokuzithanda
Uyihlo ukho
Kukuzixabisa, ubunene nentlonipho
Senjenje ke thina'ph'ekhapha
Uqine sebekufaka'meva uvelis'ama-Apile
Ubesisinyanya, sebekugawula ubafudumeze
Ubanik'umlilo
Ndim umnikazi walentsimi
Kodwa isiqhamo sayo sotyiwa ziintlanga ngeentlanga
Abanye bozithathela ngolunya
Phambi kokuba ndikuthumele eziizweni ndikuvuna ngalamazwi:
Umthi we-Apile awusoz'uvelis'amaqunube
Nowamaqunube ungasoz'uvelis'ama-Apile

Imbewu yomnqathe ayisoz'ivelis'ikhaphetshu
Neyekhaphetshu ayisoz'ivelis'umnqathe
Kudala bekulambele, bakulindele
Ngamabhozo, amacephe neembiza
Isidlo sabo asipheleli ngaphandle kwakho
Uz'ufike nakwesosixeko uyandis'imbewu yakho
Uyayazi lendawo
Sowusuka kuyo

CONTRIBUTORS

AVIWE GWELE is an original member of the CYPHER. He's participated in the 2015 Cape Town Poetry Slam where he took third place. He was also part of the exchange program with youth poets from Split This Rock, a Washington DC-based organisation. He featured in the production, *Imbewu Yesini*, and hosted "Youth Voices in Performance" at the 2016 Open Book Festival. Aviwe is fascinated by literature studies and plans to pursue it in the near future.

MOLUPI LEPEDI is a writer and performance poet from Matatiele, Eastern Cape. He began writing and performing in 2014. His work is written and performed in isiXhosa and seSotho. Molupi is one of the original members of the CYPHER program and has featured in two poetry productions. Molupi is currently the KACF bi-annual slam runner-up. He is affiliated with REPETWAH. He has also performed at the Open Book Festival.

SISIPHO MAKAMBI is a young poet from Masiphumelele, a small township near Fish Hoek. She has been writing for three years and has featured in two productions, *Ndikhululeni* and *Imbewu Yesini*. She has performed on radio, at open mics, at school and community events. Her first big break in poetry so far has been joining the CYPHER.

PALESA MOHLALA is a young poet from Cape Town. She started writing poetry in 2011 and began performing in 2013. She writes about past experiences and issues that we face as a society. Palesa's poetry has enabled her to travel abroad to England and China. She was a finalist in the Poetry For Life competition in 2015. She has performed in various places throughout Cape Town.

LESEGO MKHIZE is a Cape Town-based poet, who started writing in high school. Currently doing her first year in journalism, Lesego's first break though was as a finalist at Showville. She has featured as a guest poet at the 2015 McGregor Poetry Festival and in the *Whispers of the Heart* anthology (2015). In 2016, she shared the stage with Lingua Franca during a City Walks performance, and featured in both of CYPHER'S 2016 productions.

VUSUMUZI MPOFU is a Zimbabwean-born writer and performance poet residing in Kraaifontein. His work focuses on personal experiences and how it relates to the world. Vusumuzi is a resident poet at REPETWAH and an original member of the CYPHER. He appeared in the 2016 *English Alive* schools Anthology and featured in the 2016 Open Book Festival and Exposit Show. Vusumuzi has won multiple poetry slams around Cape Town.

SIPHOSETHU PHIKELELA is a poet from Knysna who started writing at age 13. She has featured in two CYPHER poetry-theatre productions, *Ndikhululeni* and *Imbewu Yesini*. She is the winner of the 2016 Open Book Festival and KACF poetry slams. Siphosethu is published in *Sparkling Women*, a publication which highlights women in sports, art and community activism. She writes exclusively in isiXhosa and believes everyone should feel free in expressing themselves in the language they are most comfortable with.

PHELISA SIKWATA is a young poet born and raised in Mfuleni, Cape Town. She has been writing since the age of 14 and never stopped since. Her greatest highlight thus far has been writing her 100th piece, which assured her that she is a writer who cannot live without this art. Phelisa has featured at the 2015 Cape Town Youth Poetry Slam, the 2016 CYPHER Showcase, *Ndikhululeni* (2016) and *Imbewu Yesini* (2016).

GENEVIEVE ZONGOLO is a poet from Victoria West in the Northern Cape. She has featured in the 2014 InZync Poetry Slam, the 2016 Naked Word Festival, and the 2016 Open Book Festival. She is also a 3rd year Law student at the Unisa's Parow Campus and works as an Environmentalist at the Youth Jobs in Waste Program in Stellenbosch.

POETRY FOR THE PEOPLE

ℰℒ

ALSO AVAILABLE:

Modern Rasputin by **Rosa Lyster**

Prunings by **Helen Moffett**

Questions for the Sea by **Stephen Symons**

Failing Maths and My Other Crimes by **Thabo Jijana**
WINNER OF THE 2016 INGRID JONKER PRIZE FOR POETRY

Matric Rage by **Genna Gardini**
COMMENDED FOR THE 2016 INGRID JONKER PRIZE FOR POETRY

the myth of this is that we're all in this together by **Nick Mulgrew**

ℰℒ

AVAILABLE IN 2017:

Thungachi by **Francine Simon**

Collective Amnesia by **Koleka Putuma**

ℰℒ

AVAILABLE FROM GOOD BOOKSTORES IN SOUTH AFRICA
& ELSEWHERE FROM THE AFRICAN BOOKS COLLECTIVE,
IN PRINT AND DIGITAL

ℰℒ

UHLANGAPRESS.CO.ZA

Printed in the United States
By Bookmasters